BUSINESS
U.K.

BUSINESS U.K.

A Practical Guide to Understanding British Business Culture

Peggy Kenna   Sondra Lacy

Printed on recyclable paper

PASSPORT BOOKS
a division of *NTC Publishing Group*
Lincolnwood, Illinois USA

Library of Congress Cataloging-in-Publication Data

Kenna, Peggy.
    Business U.K.: a practical guide to understanding British
business culture / Peggy Kenna, Sondra Lacy.
        p.   cm.
    ISBN 0-8442-3560-1 (pbk.)
    1. Business etiquette—Great Britain.   2. Corporate culture—Great
    Britain.   3. Business communication—Great Britain.   4. Negotiation
    in business—Great Britain.   I. Lacy, Sondra.   II. Title.
HF5389.K459   1995
395' .52'0941—dc20   94-17745
                                                          CIP

Published by Passport Books, a division of NTC Publishing Group.
4255 West Touhy Avenue, Lincolnwood, (Chicago) Illinois 60646-1975, U.S.A.
©1995 by NTC Publishing Group. All rights reserved.
No part of this work may be reproduced, stored in a retrieval system
or transmitted in any form or by any means,
electronic or mechanical, including photocopying and recording or otherwise
without the prior permission of NTC Publishing Group.
Manufactured in the United States of America.

4 5 6 7 8 9 0 VP 9 8 7 6 5 4 3 2 1

Contents

Peggy Kenna is a communications specialist working with foreign-born professionals in the American workplace. She provides cross-cultural training and consultation services to companies conducting business internationally. She is also a certified speech and language pathologist who specializes in accent modification. Peggy lives in Tempe, Arizona.

Sondra Lacy is a certified communications specialist and teaches American communication skills to foreign-born professionals in the American workplace. She also provides cross-cultural training and consultation services to companies conducting business internationally. Sondra lives in Scottsdale, Arizona.

Business U.K. is an invaluable tool for thousands of entrepreneurs, businesspeople, corporate executives, technicians, and salespeople seeking to develop lasting business relationships in the U.K.

The book provides a fast, easy way for you to become acquainted with business practices and protocol to help you increase your chances for success in the United Kingdom. You will discover the secrets of doing business internationally while improving your interpersonal communication skills.

Let this book work for you.

> Pam Del Duca
> President/CEO
> The DELSTAR Group
> Scottsdale, Arizona

Entrepreneur Of The Year®
Award Recipient

Business U.K. offers a smooth and problem-free transition between the American and British business cultures.

This pocket-size book contains information you need when traveling in the U.K. or doing business with British colleagues. It explains the differences in business culture you will encounter in such areas as:

- Business etiquette

- Communication style

- Problem solving and decision making

- Meetings and presentation style

Business U.K. gets you started on the right track and challenges you to seek ways to improve your success in the global marketplace by understanding cultural differences in the ways people communicate and do business with each other.

Successful international companies are able to adapt to the business styles acceptable in other countries and by other nationalities, based on their knowledge and awareness of key cultural differences. These differences, if not acknowledged and addressed, can interfere in successful communication and can adversely affect the success of any business attempting to expand internationally.

Business U.K. is designed to overcome such difficulties by comparing the American culture with the culture of the United Kingdom. Identifying appropriate behavior in one's own culture can make it easier to adapt to that of the country with which you are doing business. With this in mind, the book's unique parallel layout allows an at-a-glance comparison of British business practices with those of the United States.

Practical and easy to use, *Business U.K.* will help you win the confidence of British associates and achieve common business goals.

The global business environment today is a multicultural one. While general business considerations are essentially the same the world over, business styles differ greatly from country to country. What is customary and appropriate in one country may be considered unusual or even offensive in another. The increasingly competitive environment calls for an individual approach to each national market. The success of your venture outside your home market depends largely upon preparation. The American style of business is not universally accepted. Yet we send our employees, executives, salespeople, technicians to negotiate or carry out contracts with little or no understanding of the cultural differences in the ways people communicate and do business with each other. How many business deals have been lost because of this cultural myopia?

Globalization is a process which is drawing people together from all nations of the world into a single community linked by the vast network of communication technologies. Technological breakthroughs in the past two decades have made instant communication between individuals around the world an affordable reality.

The Global Marketplace

As these technological advances continue to open up and expand the dialogue among members of the world community, the need for effective communication between nations and peoples has accelerated.

When change occurs as dramatically and rapidly as we have witnessed in the past decade, many people throughout the world are being forced to quickly learn and adapt to unfamiliar ways of doing things. Some actually welcome change and the opportunities it presents, while others are reluctant to give up familiar ways of doing things. History proves that cultures are slow to change. But, individuals who are mentally prepared to accept change and deal with differences can successfully adapt to cultures very different from their own.

A culture develops when individuals have common experiences and share their reactions to these experiences by communicating with other members of their society.

Over time, communication becomes the vehicle by which cultural beliefs and values are developed, shared, and transmitted from one generation to the next. Communication and culture are mutually dependent.

Effective communication between governments or international businesses requires more than being able to speak the language fluently or relying on expert interpreters. Understanding the language is only the first step. Understanding and accepting the behaviors, customs, and attitudes of other cultures while interacting globally is also required to bring harmony and success in the worldwide business and political arena.

The importance of the influence of one's native culture on the way one approaches life cannot be overstated. Each country's cultural beliefs and values are reflected in its people's idea of the "right" way to live and behave.

In general, American businessmen and businesswomen who practice low-key, non-adversarial, win/win techniques in doing business abroad tend to be most successful. Knowing what your company wants to achieve — its bottom line — and also understanding the objectives of the other party and helping to accommodate them in the business transaction is necessary for developing long-term, international business relationships.

Often representatives from American companies have difficulty doing business with each other, even when they speak the same language and share a common culture. Consider how much more difficult it is to do business with people from different cultures who speak different languages.

Success in the international business arena will not be easy for Americans who do not take steps to gain the skills necessary to be a global player. The language barrier is an obvious problem.

Equally important will be negotiation skills, as well as an understanding of and adaptation to the social and business etiquette of the foreign country. Americans have a reputation for failing to appreciate this. In other words, American businessmen and businesswomen doing business abroad will get off to a good start if they remember to do the following:

- Listen closely; understand the verbal and non verbal communications.
- Focus on mutual interests, not differences.
- Nurture long-term relationships.
- Emphasize quality. Be prepared to defend the quality of your products and services, and the quality of your business relationship.

Fast becoming a universal passport for doing business in Europe is ISO 9000. ISO stands for International Organization for Standardization.

There is a new set of concise standards covering documented quality control systems for product development, design, production, management, and inspection.

The European Economic Community (EEC) has adopted ISO certification and more than 20,000 European companies are complying. Increasing numbers of European companies are refusing to do business with foreign suppliers who don't meet ISO standards. Product areas under the most pressure to comply include automotive, aerospace, electronics, testing and measuring instruments, and products where safety and liability can become an issue. Companies with Total Quality Management (TQM) in place find it easier to pass ISO 9000 audits.

Successful companies will need to adapt to these rules and standards set by Europe in order to do business there.

Total Quality Management is becoming an integral part of successful companies in the United States.

TQM is an organized, company-wide effort to eliminate waste in every aspect of business and to produce the highest quality product possible. TQM is a philosophy that focuses on the customer, manages by facts, empowers people, and improves processes.

Implementation of the process is a real challenge and requires a company commitment to invest the time and finances necessary to reshape the entire organization. How is this accomplished? Through a team approach which values customer and employee opinions and in which everyone is committed to identify waste and its root cause and correct it in a timely manner. An effective tool for accomplishing this is through brainstorming efforts allowing everyone to participate. The successful TQM company is customer driven and uses leadership, information and analysis, strategic quality planning, human resource utilization, and quality assurance of products and services to reach goals.

Total Quality Management is a survival tool for businesses in a global market.

Great Britain consists of England, Scotland, and Wales. When Northern Ireland is added, the correct name is United Kingdom.

Since World War II, the U.K. has given up control of history's largest empire. It is still currently redefining its current role in world affairs. Its traditional economic strength was in heavy industry but now the nation is increasingly service oriented. London is a major world financial center, and the U.K. is the largest foreign investor in the United States.

The U.K. is a very efficient and mechanized agricultural producer, and is also a major offshore petroleum producer. It is still struggling to integrate into the European Economic Community.

Americans should not assume that the British are just like them because they seem to speak the same language and seem to share a common heritage. Centuries of civilization and empire building have given the British a certain pride and assurance. Even though their current position in the world's economic and geopolitical scene has diminished, they still exercise considerable global influence through their network of commonwealth nations.

The British are far more experienced in international affairs than Americans. This is due in part to the fact that they are a relatively small island looking outward to gather news from around the world.

The British value their free time and in general seem to be content with fewer material possessions than Americans. They tend to be antagonistic to the American view of money-making and profits, efficiency and cost effectiveness. They are also much more reserved in business.

Although American women can find an acceptable business climate in Britain, the Old Boy Network is still very much alive. Sometime it is the best educated men who have the most difficulty relating to women in business. While women make up almost half of the work force, few of them have made it into senior management positions.

IMPORTANT: Remember that within a culture, there are still individual differences among people and within business organizations.

United States

■ *Outgoing and gregarious*

Americans are a very friendly and informal people but these traits can sometimes seem overly familiar and intrusive to others. Americans also tend to be very open in their relationships. They usually share family and work experiences easily. The design of most American offices encourages peer/colleague interaction. But Americans do tend to avoid close personal relationships in business.

They like to talk about themselves, their family, etc. They ask questions about each other's life and family to be friendly.

■ *Like innovation and change*

Americans tend to see change as good, although constant change causes established hierarchies and relationships to be repeatedly disrupted. The needs of the individual are subsidiary to the organization. Loyalty between employee and company is temporary but expected to be wholehearted while it lasts.

America was developed by risk takers and this trait is still highly valued. They feel that new is good and creativity is generally rewarded.

United Kingdom

■ *Polite and reserved*

The British have traditionally had a restrained style although the new generation is becoming more assertive. They don't like too much "gung ho" optimism and feel Americans can be too blunt. They want a relationship where the other party is friendly but doesn't get extremely personal or want to know about the other's business.

The British are often fairly aloof at work. They feel many of the questions Americans ask are nosy. They believe in "minding your own business" and have a strong sense of privacy.

The further north you go, the friendlier the people and the more readily they accept strangers.

■ *Like stability and tradition*

Traditionally the British have not liked speculative thinking or theorizing, but have preferred tradition, precedent, and common sense. They like the useful and practical rather than the innovative. They respect an objective, logical, and calm approach in discussions and don't like aggressiveness and high-pressure or hard-sell methods.

The British tend toward the traditional and a "We've always done it this way" attitude. They are not partial to improvising or taking risks. The British are very pragmatic which can sometimes lead them to become cynical and skeptical.

United States

■ *Like choices*

Americans believe choices should not be limited. They use the communication process for business to determine the best choices. Americans are usually willing to risk failure; they can change plans quickly since they usually have alternative plans ready to put in place.

■ *Optimistic*

Obstacles can be challenges for Americans who are great believers in the possibilities for success.

■ *Like numbers and statistics*

Many Americans feel that the most reliable facts are those in the form of quantities such as specific numbers, percentages, rates, rankings, or amounts. They feel that quoting statistics gives credibility to their statements.

■ *Dislike choices*

As an island nation, consumer choices have been limited; so it has been more difficult to launch new products. British consumers tend to believe choices should be limited; they are happier when they know what is expected. They tend to be people of fixed habits and to dislike the impromptu because of a fear of the unknown.

■ *Pessimistic*

The British don't tend to be an optimistic people. Obstacles are often seen as major and they have a great fear of showing ignorance. It can be hard to get them to try something new. However, under conditions of truly great adversity, they respond well.

■ *More imprecise*

The British often avoid definitive statements. A polite request in business may be a demand or a way of telling you how to do something. When someone says "sorry" it can mean anything from an apology to expressing anger or indignation. They also avoid direct confrontation and argument. The British convey displeasure very subtly. Statements such as "Did you really..." or "I'm surprised that..." indicate that they disapprove of your tactics.

United States

■ *Individual decision makers*

One person is usually given power to make the final decision and bear all responsibility. Decisions tend to go from the top down. However, decision makers are found at all levels depending on the importance of the decision. Lower levels often get a chance to provide input. Americans believe that those closest to a problem should have input in determining the solution.

■ *Teams*

Americans have traditionally used teamwork rather than group consensus. However, Total Quality Management has lead a number of companies to implement a consensus approach to problem solving. Teams are both competitive and cooperative; there is communication between teams as well as individual accounting by and within teams.

■ *Consensus oriented*

British dislike taking the initiative. A leader's job is to build a consensus and establish good relationships between management and workers. Instructions are usually disguised as requests.

British don't like "take charge" and aggressive people.

■ *Teams*

The British like working in teams. Individual British are uncomfortable taking the initiative; they want the consensus of a team behind them. There is a strong feeling for individual accountability in implementation. When something goes wrong, they look for the culprit. They have a strong sense of fair play.

United States

■ *Status*

Americans believe but don't always practice the idea that every person — no matter what rank or status — has the potential for leadership.

■ *Open*

Information disseminated within a company rarely remains a secret but becomes news to the "outside" very quickly.

■ *Decision making*

All people are expected to express opinions openly, and the majority rules. Final decision making has parameters within each management level. Empowerment at each level is understood as to its limits.

■ *Status*

Formal rank and status matter a lot. The British have a tradition of public service. In the past many have believed that natural leaders, not self-made men and women, should be the ones to govern or to run business. The principle of the Labour Party, born out of the trade unions, is to give lower-born people the same opportunity to lead.

■ *Secretive with outsiders*

Information is disseminated within a company but the British tend to be very secretive about business matters with outsiders.

■ *Decision making*

Because they dislike change and taking risks, it can take a long time to come to a decision. Decision making is usually the prerogative of senior management. This contributes to dislike of reform and change; they tend to be cautious. Fear of failure or loss of a management job is a major personal stigma. Unions have input at the plant-level work environment.

United Sates

■ *Directive management*

There are still companies in which the "Old Boy Network" is very strong, but mid-size and smaller companies are becoming more successful using directive management with broader matrixes of leadership.

In larger American companies someone is always in charge and there is a clear decision maker. Americans have little concept of shared responsibility. Whoever is put in charge of implementing a decision is expected to be completely accountable for its success or failure.

American colleges and universities in the last decade have graduated a large number of business majors, so there is no shortage of professionally educated managers.

■ *Planning*

In recent years American companies are adjusting to the fast-changing world business scene and, therefore, short-term planning with lots of options and flexibility are becoming norms for survival.

Americans tend to be both strategic and tactical planners. Business contracts are written, detailed, and not very flexible. Any changes need to be renegotiated. Planning tends to be fairly short term.

United Kingdom

■ *Top down hierarchies*

The "Old Boy Network" and class system are still very strong in the U.K. Boards of directors tend to be the principal decision-making units.

The British have tended to feel managers should have experience and character rather than science and skill. Privatization of many industries is changing this attitude.

Higher-level executives still usually have a good educational and social background. Lower- and middle-level managers are more likely to have come up through the ranks.

There is a serious shortage of professionally educated managers, so recently all levels of management have been sent to specific courses on decision making.

■ *Planning*

The British engage in much national economic planning, but planning can be weak at the company level. They prefer pragmatism over theory and opportunism over planning. Final decisions tend to be made at the top. Due to a changing economic and political scene, their outlook is mostly short term.

United States

■ *Constant change*

Constant change causes social hierarchies and relationships to be repeatedly disrupted. The needs of the individual are subsidiary to the organization. Loyalty between employee and company is temporary but expected to be wholehearted. Americans will probably give a new idea a fair hearing and everyone wants to be the leader with a new product or service.

Americans are future oriented. They tend to make decisions more quickly and easily. While accuracy is important, errors are tolerated. They believe you learn from failure and should take risks. Criticism is objective; tact, however, is important. Risk taking and competition are primary methods of motivation.

■ *Systematic*

Americans like to work within a rational and systematic framework, but they also like to have options and flexibility. Since risk taking is rewarded and failure as well as success is considered reality, American companies tend to move quickly with implementation of plans that are well thought-out.

United Kingdom

■ *Don't like change*

Typically the British are not risk takers. They tend to look at past performance as a guide rather than look at accounting projections on the success of new methods. It is important to emphasize immediate as well as long-term benefits. They are less inclined to be interested in change, novelty, or innovation than in continuity and stability. They are also less likely to be interested in a new product just because it is new. The British can have the attitude that it is better not to try so you don't risk failure. A good but new idea may not always get a hearing.

Oral agreements are binding.

■ *"Muddle through"*

British have an aversion to working within a rational and systematic framework; they prefer to go slow, get by, manage somehow.

United States

■ *Tend to be impatient*

Americans are usually very punctual because time is equated with money. The day is divided into segments to be completed. There is a beginning and ending time for each section of the day.

■ *Workaholics*

Americans are seen as packing every moment with business (power breakfasts, etc.). Americans are also seen as lacking the ability to relax or do nothing, even in their own personal lives. They appear to run their lives like a business.

In general Americans tend to work longer and harder than most Europeans. Sometimes even an average worker is seen as a person with an extraordinary commitment to the task.

■ *Patient*

The British are not clock watchers like Americans are. They dislike rushing about and constant activity. A slower-paced lifestyle is valued. On social occasions it is not unusual for people to arrive 15–20 minutes late. However, in business they like punctuality.

■ *Value personal time*

The British feel that business and personal time should be more separate. They don't like to combine meals with business, for example.

United States

■ *Communication tool*

Some meetings are to brainstorm for ideas; some are to disseminate information; some are to make decisions.

Americans like to get right down to business since meetings are usually tightly scheduled and have a fixed agenda. A meeting may be adjourned before all business is completed.

Meetings can become very heated with a number of confrontations and disagreements to be resolved.

■ *Both formal and informal*

There are several types of meetings in American companies. They can be formal meetings in which information is disseminated. Or they can be informal brainstorming sessions in which questions are asked, heated arguments take place, and decisions are made. Everyone is free to express his or her own opinion, and the majority rules.

United Kingdom

■ *Management tool*

Meetings are very frequent since they are an important tool for managers to build consensus.

The British also like to get down to business quickly and like to have an agenda.

■ *Informal style*

Opinions are encouraged from everyone, but seniority gives extra weight. Building passive consensus is very important.

United States

■ *Action oriented*

While Americans like to debate, they are primarily concerned with the results of a meeting and like to have action items assigned to participants.

Everyone is encouraged to present opinions and then the majority rules. Tlhe group tends to stick to the issue and becomes impatient with digressions.

■ *Presentations*

Americans tend to have a projecting style of presentation. They will often combine informative and persuasive styles as an efficient method of presentation. They attempt to persuade the audience to make a decision or take an action at the same time as they provide information. They consider this an effective and efficient use of time. Americans also believe in the "hard sell" and "quick close" approach to selling. They expect the audience to ask questions and to test the presenter's knowledge. Presenters expect to defend their opinions.

United Kingdom

■ *Want concrete results*

Almost all decisions are formulated, discussed, approved, ratified, communicated, and implemented at a meeting. A meeting without concrete results is seen as a failure. Most information is shared at meetings.

■ *Presentations*

Presentations should be matter-of-fact, complete in technical or marketing detail, and understated. They shouldn't be overly demonstrative, enthusiastic, or emotional and should avoid any comparisons to the U.S. It is best not to do most of the talking and to refrain from using American idioms such as "bottom line," "ASAP," etc.

The British will need time to make a decision so they probably won't give immediate feedback. They like to have some material left behind to look at. British executives will pay attention to details and will want to analyze information thoroughly.

Terms such as "We are excited about..." sound frivolous to the British.

United States

■ *Competitive*

Americans are very competitive and want to get the best deal. However, Americans can be fairly flexible in order to conclude a business transaction.

Americans do little bargaining in the area of price. They often bargain in areas such as delivery dates, etc. Their initial demands are usually close to what they believe to be fair and reasonable.

Americans believe you must negotiate from a strength position.

■ *Impatient*

Decisions are often made quickly. Not all decisions need to be made by executives; sometimes lower-level managers can make decisions. Sometimes their impatience to complete negotiations can lead Americans to make unnecessary concessions.

Punctuality is important. Americans will seldom be more than a few minutes late to a meeting or negotiation session. They also expect others to be equally punctual.

United Kingdom

■ *Tough*

British operate under a burden of conflicting political and economic demands as well as an excess of restrictions and union pressures. But they tend to be tough, even ruthless, negotiators; they are firm at the bargaining table.

Bargaining is not a usual fact of everyday life for the British. It is best to leave room for movement but not build a large amount of "fat" into a proposal. The British tend to have moderate initial demands.

They pay attention to formalities and protocol, especially in London.

■ *Fairly fast pace*

The pace of negotiations is fairly fast but somewhat slower than in the U.S. The British don't tend to bargain much but do like to have some concessions. They don't like people who push for agreement or appear in a hurry. High pressure tactics are viewed as negative.

Punctuality is very important; the British also value patience.

United States

■ *Delivery*

Americans are becoming more conscious of "on time" delivery as the customer satisfaction issues surface. Even so, promises are sometimes ahead of practices. They try to be "on time" as the ideal.

■ *More spontaneous*

They also tend to be more spontaneous in their approach to negotiations rather than engaging in a lot of planning. They are often fairly informal in their approach to negotiations.

People are trusted to perform in an environment where authority assigns responsibility and actions are measured.

Younger managers with modern management training do tend to be more aggresssive.

■ *Extroverts*

American negotiators have a reputation for being emotional and potentially explosive when negotiating. They can become very argumentative and confrontive.

Americans do not tend to learn other languages, but they do not usually assume everyone speaks English.

United Kingdom

■ *Delivery*

The British have had a serious problem with late delivery of products. They have spent much effort trying to deal with this problem but it stubbornly refuses to go away.

■ *Disciplined approach*

The British work in teams and there is much prior discussion as to tactics and stand to take. Younger executives with modern management training and technical background are much more aggressive than older negotiators. The British are very technically competent and produce highly-inventive scientific and engineering people.

■ *Reserved*

British negotiators tend not to exert much energy. They have a take-it-or-leave-it attitude. Their approach to negotiations is more formal and diplomatic.

Providing them with information that aids them in analyzing a proposal gives the best chance for success.

The British do not tend to learn other languages since they assume everyone speaks English.

United States

■ *Negotiators*

The people who are negotiating for their company or business have usually already been notified by high-level executives before the meeting of the expected agreement/outcome of the meeting.

Americans do not like to spend time building relationships, but get right down to business. They do this from a desire not to waste time.

Americans want to accomplish the job with a minimum expenditure of time and effort.

■ *Open*

Americans tend to be very open and direct in their communication. They like to deal with differences directly and tend to "lay their cards on the table" in order to resolve issues.

■ *Agreements*

Americans are legalistic and like detailed contracts with all contingencies spelled out. These contracts tend to be fairly inflexible and are expected to be adhered to.

■ *Negotiators*

British negotiators increasingly come from a technical background. Most British negotiators are less competitive in style than U.S. negotiators.

The British do not like to spend time building relationships, but get right down to business. They do this from a desire not to get involved.

The British are very practical and like to have details stressed and the practical implications of a proposal within the long-term picture highlighted and explained. Use a disciplined approach; be restrained.

■ *"Economical with the truth"*

The British do not lay their cards on the table. They are not always open and direct. They tend to phrase negative remarks in tentative sounding language. They also prefer giving information in writing so the other person can look at it privately.

■ *Agreements*

Negotiations often conclude with an oral agreement and a handshake. They take this very seriously; the written agreement comes later. Agreements contain much detail, and decisions only come from upper management.

U.S. Business Etiquette

- Be punctual. Americans are very time conscious. They also tend to conduct business at a
  fairly fast pace.

- A firm handshake and direct eye contact is the
  standard greeting.

- Direct eye contact is very important in business.
  Not making eye contact implies boredom or
  disinterest.

- Gift giving is not common. The U.S. has
  bribery laws which restrict the value of gifts
  which can be given.

- The U.S. is not particularly rank and status conscious. Titles are not used when addressing
  executives. Americans usually like to use first
  names very quickly. Informality tends to be
  equated with equality.

- Business meetings usually start with a formal
  agenda and tasks to be accomplished. There is
  usually very little small talk. Participants are
  expected to express their ideas openly; disagreements are common.

- Permission should be asked before smoking.

- It is common to discuss business over breakfast, lunch, or dinner. Also, some business deals are still concluded on the golf course.

- Business dress is basically conservative but gets more informal the further west you go.

- Decision making is actually decentralized and dispersed among many individuals and groups. It is important to find out who has final authority. Decision making tends to be quick.

- Many women hold middle-management positions in the United States and a steadily growing number are in top executive positions. The same courtesy and respect should be shown women as men in business. Special or traditional courtesies such as opening doors are not always appreciated by women executives.

- Most American businesspeople carry business cards but do not automatically exchange them. They usually exchange them only if there is some reason to want to get in touch at a later time.

British Business Etiquette

- A "queue" or line is almost sacred. Never try to push your way into a line of waiting people. The British have a strong sense of privacy.

- Politeness and good manners and the appearance of self assurance are very important; the British are fairly formal.

- The British have subtle and complex class distinctions; they classify each other by speech, dress, and manners.

- The British tend to use humor a lot. British humor tends to be satirical and sarcastic. Unless you are well versed in British ways, use humor with discretion.

- Avoid personal questions. Many British find Americans pushy and intrusive in their conversation. Keep it impersonal.

- Loud conversations and any form of boisterousness in public places should be avoided.

- The British do not appreciate an exaggerated or conspicuous display of affluence. Showing off may bring a negative reaction.

- Telephones are not used as extensively in the U.K. as they are in the U.S. They do not really conduct much business over the phone except to make arrangements for a meeting.

- Be conspicuously polite to older people.

- Use "please" and "thank you" constantly. Never say "give me" or "bring me" without using "please" with it.
- Never call a Scotsman English.
- The British don't like to be called "Brits."
- When eating put both hands in sight with wrists lightly touching the edge of the table.
- Always shake hands when meeting someone.
- The British use first names fairly quickly, but it is best at the beginning of business to use a person's formal last name and title (i.e., Mister).
- Don't ask where a person went to school, as they may think you are being nosy and trying to determine their social class.
- Avoid discussing politics.
- Accountants have more prestige than lawyers.
- The British warm up to personal relationships slowly.
- Many British don't particularly consider themselves Europeans. Don't think that because you have visited in other European countries you will understand the U.K.

U.S. Gestures

- Americans tend to stand an arm's length away from each other.

- Americans generally respect queues or lines. To shove or push one's way into a line will often result in anger and verbal complaint.

- Beckoning is done by raising the index finger and curling it in and out, or by raising the hand and curling the fingers back toward the body.

- Using the hand and index finger to point at objects or to point directions is common.

- Whistling is a common way to get the attention of someone at a distance.

- "No" is signalled by waving the forearm and hand (palm out) in front and across the upper body, back and forth.

- Americans use the standard "OK" sign, the "V" for victory sign, and the thumbs-up sign.

- The "V" for victory sign is only done with the palm facing outward; otherwise it is an obscene gesture.

- Physical touching to emphasize a point or moving closer is not appropriate. The British are very sensitive to privacy.

- The British use hand gestures very sparingly, even during a presentation.

- The British also use few facial expressions. It is not polite to display anger, frustration, incredulity, or amazement.

- Do not keep your hands in your pockets when speaking.

Effective communication, both verbal and nonverbal, means that the sending and processing of information between people, countries, and businesses is understood, examined, interpreted, and responded to in some way. Any factor that causes a barrier or eliminates the successful transmission of information is defined as a communication interference.

- **Environmental interference** is an actual physical disturbance in the environment such as power outage, unregulated temperatures, a person or group talking very loudly, etc.

- **Physiological interference** is like a hearing loss, laryngitis, illness, stuttering, neurological or organic deficit, etc.

- **Semantic interference.** We understand a word to have a certain meaning but the other person has a different meaning. Body language and gestures mean different things to different people. This includes confusion of abbreviated organizational jargon and pronunciation. Universal meanings (semantic understanding) are rare.

- **Syntactic interference.** Words are placed in certain order to give our language meaning. If the words are out of order, the meaning may be changed (this includes grammar).

- **Organizational interference.** Ideas being discussed lack sequence and can't be followed.

- **Psychological interference.** Words that incite emotion are used. In any emotional state (positive or negative) emotions need to be diffused in order to communicate effectively.

- **Social interference.** This includes cultural manners that are inappropriate for the country, such as accepted codes for dress, business etiquette, communication rules, social activity.

Always become well informed about the customs and culture and get information **before** you try and do business in another country. Review this book and decide which areas of communication you and your colleagues will have difficulty with in the U.K. Anticipate and plan accordingly.

As the visitor to another country, you need to move out of your "comfort zone" as an American. Make the people from another country feel comfortable doing business with you.

No one country has a lock on world markets. Fundamental changes have occurred in the world economy in the last decade. New technologies and low labor costs often give nations that once were not major players an advantage. This results in increased competition. Yet international business is vital to any country's prosperity.

Business is conducted by people, and the future of any country in a global economy will lie with people who can effectively think and act across ethnic, cultural, and language barriers. We need to understand that the differences between nations and cultures is profound. The European-based culture of the United States has very different values and behaviors than other cultures in the world. If you cannot accept and adapt to these differences, you will not succeed.

Companies striving to market their business overseas can become truly successful only when they recognize that the key is operating with sensitivity toward the culture and communication of the other country. Communication cannot be separated from culture and this is true when doing business in other countries.

No flourishing company would present themselves to another company in the same country without researching that company's business culture and then adapting their image to meet the customer's comfort level. It's the same when doing business in another country. You must adapt your image by using your knowledge of effective cultural communication to present a positive public image to the other country.

The first thing is to identify your target audience: clients, customers, suppliers, financial people, government employees, and so on. Then you must learn how to effectively communicate with them, and this means learning the culture.

Business failure internationally rarely results from technical or professional incompetence. It is often due to a lack of understanding of what people from other countries want, how they work, and so on. This lack of understanding can put a company at a tremendous disadvantage.

Learning the business protocol and practices of the country where you want to do business can give you great leverage. The more you know about the people you do business with, the more successful you can be. Businesspeople need to make every contact they have with a foreign customer or business partner a positive one. Business leaders and managers must rethink the way they do business in the new global marketplace.

To be successful in the global market, you must:

- **Be flexible.** Adapting to differences in culture is necessary for individuals from both countries to get along and do business. Resisting the local culture will only lead to distrust.

- **Have patience.** Adjust your planning. Initiating business in many countries takes a long-range approach and may require two or three years. Anticipate problems and develop alternative strategies.

- **Prepare thoroughly.** Research the country, the organization, the culture, and beliefs of the people you will be dealing with.

- **Know your bottom line.** Know exactly what you want from a deal and at what point an agreement is not in your best interest. Know when to walk away.

- **Show respect.** Search for the other side's needs and interests. Accentuate the positive. Don't preach your own beliefs and respect their beliefs.

- **Form relationships.** Encourage getting involved with the new community if you are going to be in the country for a long period.

■ **Keep your cool**. Pay attention to the wide
range of national, cultural, religious, and social
differences you encounter.

When you are using this book, review your own
beliefs and values about correct business protocol
and ethics. Then match these ideas with the business
practices and protocol in the United Kingdom.

You can contribute to your own success by recog-
nizing that you will have to move out of your own
"comfort zone" of doing business the "American way"
into the cultural business zone of the U.K. in order
to develop the rapport necessary to meet the needs of
your client or partner. This does not mean you com-
promise your company's image or product but that
you do business following British protocol while
there. It's only for a short time that you may be following their rules, and the payoff can be one in
which concepts can be sold while still maintaining a
consistent image and approach that is culturally
appropriate.

Quick Tips: United States

- The U.S. is a very ethnically diverse country. To do business with Americans, it is important to be open to this diversity and to be flexible.

- Americans tend to be very individually oriented and concerned with their own careers. Their first loyalty is to themselves.

- Americans want to be liked. They prefer people who are good team players and want to cooperate.

- Americans value equality and dislike people who are too status or rank conscious.

- Most Americans are open, friendly, casual, and informal in their manners. They like to call people by first name quickly.

- Americans like to come right to the point and are uncomfortable with people who are indirect or subtle.

- Americans expect people to speak up and give their opinions freely and to be honest in the information they give. They like to have a specific, definite "yes" or "no."

- Americans can be very persistent. When they conclude a business transaction and sign a contract, they expect it to be honored. They do not like people who change their minds later.

- U.S. companies pride themselves on being efficient, purposeful, direct, single-minded and materialistic. The bottom line is very important.

- Americans admire aggressiveness in business. They like the dynamic pursuit of personal and corporate goals. They have an open and energetic approach to work.

- Meetings are a communication tool for imparting or gathering information. They are also a forum for formal proposals.

- Business life extends deep into family and social life in the United States.

■ Put it in writing.
The British greatly respect the printed word, mailed or faxed. Before meeting with contacts, drop them a note or introduction.

■ Cut out the glitz.
Many British managers are neither Oxford nor Cambridge graduates but come from "red brick" universities and a budget-minded background.

■ Watch your language.
The British brand of English can be different enough, at times, to cause trouble. For instance, "Let's table this matter" means to kill or postpone it to an American, but to the British it means to put it on the agenda.

■ Slow down.
The British like to ease into a business relationship by getting to know you — over tea or a drink — and by building up trust. Don't be a clock watcher.

■ Honor the hierarchy.
In your zeal to get things done quickly, don't detour around your contact. British managers still largely adhere to the chain of command more than easygoing Americans. They're very aware of "upstairs, downstairs" distinctions. Upstairs begins with the Queen.

- Avoid comparisons with the U.S.

- Make connections with the traditional power brokers. The old class system still influences business. Traditions are important.

- Make prior appointments and be punctual.

- Gift giving is common. Logo gifts with your company name should be unobtrusive. Be careful not to leave an impression that you are trying to bribe your counterpart.

- Successful products in England have retained their strong American identity and are backed by quality and service.

- The three qualities the British like are quality, service, and fun. Americans are seen as innovative, exciting, friendly, and self-indulgent. The same goes for their products.

- American products that have transferred successfully are the relatively common, everyday items that mix fun, business, and leisure.

- The British want to hear only good things about their country. It is best to listen and not become defensive when they tell you what's wrong with America.

Although Americans and British do share a common language, it would be a big mistake to assume there will be no problem in making yourself understood. Many words have different meanings and the two countries can use different terms to describe the same thing.

The original English accent is something like the modern American accent used in the mid-Atlantic states. The English accent today was developed in the last century by the upper classes to sound posh and the lower classes mimicked this.

The hardest thing to understand in another country is their humor. The British like to use verbal word play and can use humor and jokes as a secret weapon.

The British tend to be much more precise in their use of English than Americans, who rely more on context to get their meaning across.

American	British
chips	crisps
French fries	chips
cookie	biscuit
restroom	WC, toilet
billion	thousand million
chemist	druggist
first floor	ground floor
half	very much
eraser	rubber

Notes

Available in this series:

Business China

Business France

Business Germany

Business Japan

Business Mexico

Business Taiwan

Business Korea

Business Italy

Business Spain

Business U.K.

For more information, please contact:

Sales and Marketing Department
NTC Publishing Group
4255 West Touhy Avenue
Lincolnwood, IL 60646
798-679-5500